Kid Pick!

Title: _____

Author: _____

Picked by: _____

_____

Why I love this book:

_____

_____

THE MOON

EARLY BIRD
ASTRONOMY

BY LAURA HAMILTON WAXMAN

LERNER PUBLICATIONS COMPANY • MINNEAPOLIS

The images in this book are used with permission of: NASA/JPL/USGS, pp. 4, 7, 13; NASA/JSC, pp. 5, 28, 30, 31, 32, 37, 38, 39, 40, 48 (bottom); © J. Silver/SuperStock, pp. 6, 48 (top); © Pacific Stock/SuperStock, p. 8; © Science and Society/SuperStock, pp. 9, 21; NASA/JPL, p. 10; NASA/JPL/Malin Space Science Systems, p. 11; © Laura Westlund/Independent Picture Service, pp. 12, 16, 26; © Larry Chiger/SuperStock, p. 14; © Larry Landolfi/Photo Researchers, Inc., p. 15; © John W. Bova/Photo Researchers, Inc., pp. 17, 20; © Eckhard Slawik/Photo Researchers, Inc., p. 18; © Photononstop/SuperStock, pp. 19, 43; © age fotostock/SuperStock, pp. 22, 34; © Digital Zoo/Photodisc/Getty Images, p. 23; © Gunnar Kullenberg/SuperStock, p. 24; © Tom Fowlks/Taxi/ Getty Images, p. 25; © Michael P. Gadomski/Photo Researchers, Inc., p. 27 (both); © StockTrek/ Photodisc/Getty Images, p. 29; © Robert Harding/Digital Vision/Getty Images, p. 33; © Hulton Archive/Getty Images, p. 35; NASA/KSC, p. 36; AP Photo/NASA, Jack Pfaller, p. 41; © Chris Butler/Photo Researchers, Inc., p. 42; © Barry Blackman/SuperStock, p. 46; © NovaStock/ SuperStock, p. 47.

Front Cover: NASA/JPL (main); NASA, ESA, and The Hubble Heritage Team (STScl/AURA), Y. Momany (University of Padma) (background).
Back Cover: NASA, ESA, and The Hubble Heritage Team (STScl/AURA).

Lerner Publications Company
A division of Lerner Publishing Group, Inc.
241 First Avenue North
Minneapolis, MN 55401 U.S.A.

Website address: www.lernerbooks.com

Library of Congress Cataloging-in-Publication Data

Waxman, Laura Hamilton.
    The moon / by Laura Hamilton Waxman.
        p.   cm. — (Early bird astronomy)
    Includes index.
    ISBN 978–0–7613–3872–7 (lib. bdg. : alk. paper)
    1. Moon—Juvenile literature. I. Title.
    QB582.W39 2010
    523.3—dc22   2009022101

Manufactured in the United States of America
1 – BP – 12/15/09

CONTENTS

BE A WORD DETECTIVE

Can you find these words as you read about the Moon? Be a detective and try to figure out what they mean. You can turn to the glossary on page 46 for help.

astronauts	gravity	spacecraft
astronomers	orbit	telescope
atmosphere	phases	tide
axis	rotate	waning moon
eclipse	solar system	waxing moon

Stars twinkle around the Moon at sunset. Why does the Moon look bigger than the stars?

CHAPTER 1
BIG AND BRIGHT

Look up at the sky on a clear night. What do you see? Thousands of stars are shining. You may spot a planet or two. But on most nights, the Moon shines biggest and brightest of all.

The Moon does not make its own light. It reflects light from the Sun. And it isn't really bigger than stars or planets. It just looks bigger.

Close objects look bigger than faraway objects. The Moon is closer to Earth than any planets or stars. So the Moon looks big in our sky. But the Moon is a lot smaller than distant stars and planets. It is smaller than our home planet too. Nearly fifty Moons could fit inside Earth.

In this image, photographs of Earth and the Moon were put together to show that the Moon is much smaller than Earth.

The Moon glows over Honolulu, Hawaii.

You can see the Moon easily on most nights. It is covered with light and dark patches. Some people think the dark patches look like a face. Other people see a rabbit or wolf.

8

You can get a better look at the Moon with a telescope (TEH-luh-skohp). Telescopes make faraway objects look bigger and closer. A telescope shows that the Moon's surface is not smooth. It has high places and low places. It has flat places and bumpy places.

This picture was taken through a telescope. It shows the bumps and wrinkles on the Moon's surface.

This picture combines photos of the eight planets near the Sun. Is Earth the only planet that has a moon?

CHAPTER 2

EARTH'S NEAREST NEIGHBOR

Earth and the Moon are both part of the solar system. The solar system includes the Sun and eight planets. The Sun lies at the center of the solar system.

Most of the planets have at least one moon.
A moon is an object that circles a planet in space.
Earth has just one moon. Our moon is about
238,855 miles (384,400 kilometers) away from
Earth. Imagine a rope that long. It could wrap
around Earth more than nine times. But the
Moon is still our closest neighbor in space. The
Sun is almost four hundred times farther away.

This picture of Earth and the Moon was taken from space, near the planet Mars.

The Moon is always moving. It follows a path around Earth called an orbit. The Moon takes about 27 days to complete one orbit.

The Moon also rotates (ROH-tayts). It spins around like a top. The Moon rotates on its axis (AK-sihs). An axis is an imaginary line that goes through the center of the Moon from top to bottom. The Moon takes about 27 days to rotate once.

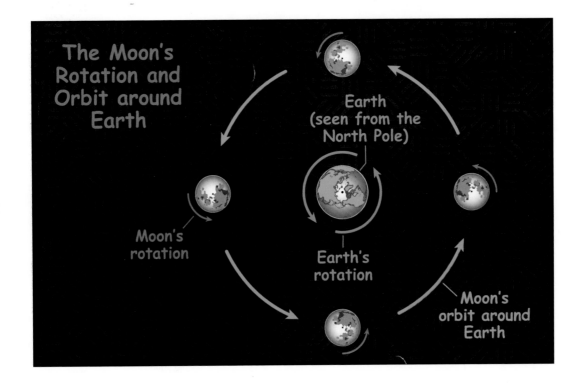

The Moon's Rotation and Orbit around Earth

Earth (seen from the North Pole)

Moon's rotation

Earth's rotation

Moon's orbit around Earth

This picture shows the far side of the Moon. This side is never visible from Earth.

The Moon rotates and travels its orbit in the same amount of time. This timing makes something interesting happen. It causes the same part of the Moon to always face Earth, even as the Moon spins. So we always see the same side of the Moon. The side we see is called the near side. The side we never see is called the far side.

The Moon does not always look round. What are the Moon's different shapes called?

CHAPTER 3
THE CHANGING MOON

The Moon does not look the same each night. It seems to change shape. Its different shapes are called phases.

You can see the Moon's phases for yourself. Go outside on a clear night. Look at the Moon. Draw the shape that you see. Repeat this every night for a week. Then look at all your drawings. Has the Moon gotten bigger or smaller?

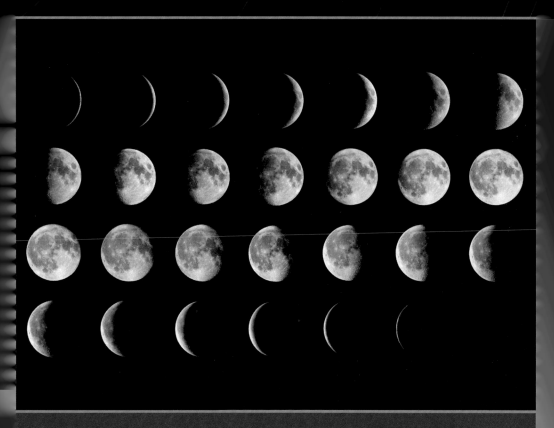

This series of pictures shows the phases of the Moon over twenty-eight nights in a row.

The Moon's shape is not really changing. So what causes its phases? Remember, the Moon follows an orbit around Earth. So the Moon is in a different place in space each night. That means sunlight shines on a different part of the Moon each night. We see only the part of the Moon's near side that the Sun lights up.

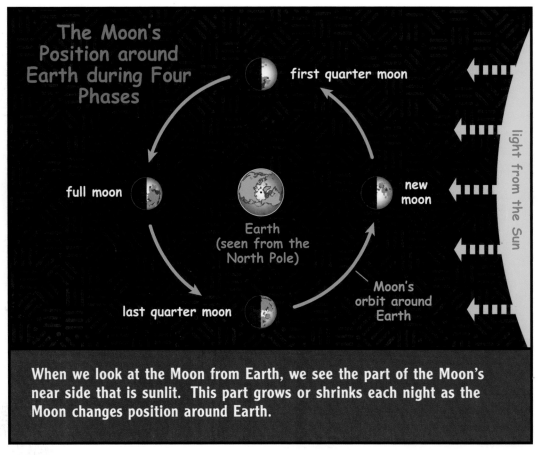

The Moon's Position around Earth during Four Phases

first quarter moon

full moon

Earth (seen from the North Pole)

new moon

Moon's orbit around Earth

last quarter moon

light from the Sun

When we look at the Moon from Earth, we see the part of the Moon's near side that is sunlit. This part grows or shrinks each night as the Moon changes position around Earth.

The Moon takes about a month to go through all of its phases. The first phase is called a new moon. During a new moon, the Moon is between the Sun and Earth. Sunlight shines only on the Moon's far side. It does not shine on the near side. So we cannot see the Moon in the sky.

Soon after a new moon, a small part of the Moon's near side is lit up. We see a crescent moon. A crescent moon looks like the thin edge of a circle.

A waxing moon grows to show half of the Moon's near side. This is called a quarter moon. The Moon is one quarter of the way through its phases.

The Moon keeps following its orbit. Its near side gets a little more sunlight each night. So from Earth, the Moon seems to grow a little each night. A growing moon is called a waxing moon.

The Moon reaches the other side of Earth after about two weeks. Then its entire near side faces the Sun. We see it glow like a big white circle in the sky. This phase is called a full moon.

The bright glow of a full moon reflects off the ocean waves.

The Moon changes again after a full moon. Its near side gets a little less light each night. So it seems to shrink a little every night. A shrinking moon is called a waning (WAYN-ing) moon. The Moon takes about two more weeks to finish its orbit. Then it starts over again as a new moon.

A waning moon shrinks night by night.

The Moon looks orange during a lunar eclipse. A lunar eclipse happens when the Moon passes through Earth's shadow.

Sometimes Earth is lined up just right between the Sun and the Moon. Then our planet blocks most of the sunlight heading to the Moon. This nighttime event is called a lunar eclipse (ee-KLIHPS). The Moon does not look white during a lunar eclipse. It usually glows a dull orange.

The Moon blocks the Sun during a solar eclipse.

Sometimes the Moon is lined up just right between Earth and the Sun. So part of Earth lies in the shadow of a new moon. Then the Moon blocks sunlight going to our planet. This event is called a solar eclipse. The Moon looks like a dark circle in the daytime sky. Just a little sunlight shines out around the Moon's edges.

On Earth, a force pulls you down when you jump. What is this force called?

CHAPTER 4

THE POWER OF THE MOON

All objects in space have gravity. Gravity is a force that pulls one object toward another. Earth's gravity keeps people and things from floating into space. You can jump up from the ground. But gravity will always pull you back down. Earth's gravity pulls on the Moon too. It keeps the Moon from floating away like a balloon.

Earth's gravity holds the Moon close to it.

Bigger objects have more gravity than smaller ones. Earth is bigger than the Moon. So Earth's gravity is stronger. But the Moon has gravity too.

The Moon's gravity pulls on Earth's waters. It makes the oceans rise and fall each day. This rising and falling is called the tide. The ocean at its highest level is called high tide. The ocean at its lowest level is called low tide.

A woman crosses a rocky beach during low tide in Panama City, Panama. The puddles and bare sand show the places that will be covered with water at high tide.

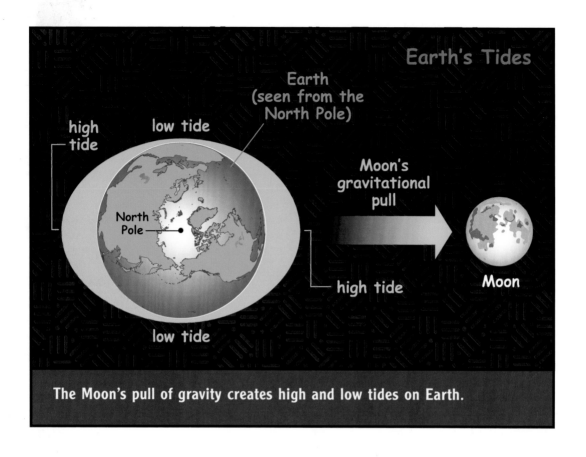

Earth
(seen from the
North Pole)

high
tide

low tide

Moon's
gravitational
pull

North
Pole

high tide

Moon

low tide

The Moon's pull of gravity creates high and low tides on Earth.

Earth's movement helps to cause the tides. Earth is always rotating. So different parts of Earth face the Moon at different times. High tide happens at the part of our planet that is turned toward the Moon. The Moon's gravity pulls hardest on that part of Earth. And the waters rise.

The tide goes out when that part of Earth is turning away from the Moon. Then the oceans sink back down to low tide. Other forces help create another high tide on the opposite side of Earth from the Moon.

TOP: At low tide, boats in this Canadian harbor float below the level of the dock. Much of the shoreline is exposed. **BOTTOM:** At high tide, the water level in the harbor is higher. The boats float near the top of the dock, and the shoreline is underwater.

On Earth, our daytime sky looks blue. This is because a layer of gases and dust around Earth scatters sunlight. What does the daytime sky look like on the Moon?

CHAPTER 5

THE MOON UP CLOSE

The Moon is a silent and still place. No plants or animals live there. It never rains or snows. No winds blow. The sky is always dark and full of stars.

Grey rocks and dust cover the Moon. The dust is powdery and thick. The Moon has many craters too. Craters are bowl-shaped pits in the ground. Some of the Moon's craters are very big. The Moon's biggest crater is 1,550 miles (2,500 km) wide. That's about half as wide as the United States.

This picture shows the side of the Moon that faces away from Earth. The far side of the Moon has many more craters than the near side. Some craters even have smaller craters inside them.

The Moon also has high mountains and deep valleys. Other places are smooth and flat. Dark rock covers these flat places. From Earth, they look like dark patches.

The flat stretches of dark rock on the Moon are called seas, because they look like Earth's seas from a distance. But they don't have any liquid water.

No plants or animals live on the Moon. It does not have the gases or water that they need to live.

The Moon has almost no atmosphere (AT-muhs-feer). An atmosphere is a layer of gases surrounding a planet. Earth's atmosphere has lots of oxygen. Humans need oxygen to breathe. The Moon has no oxygen. So people cannot breathe on the Moon.

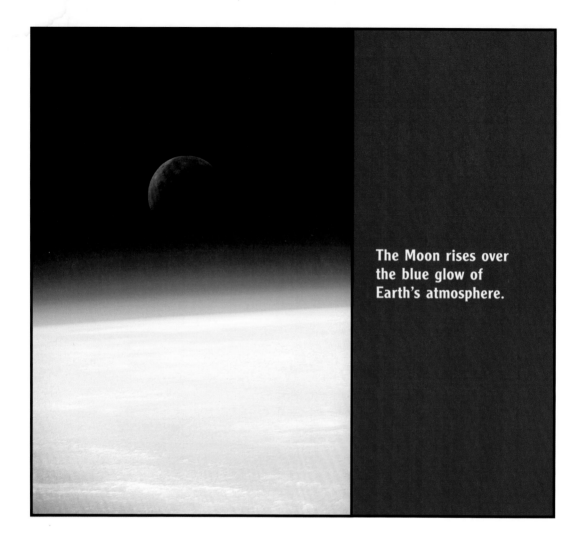

The Moon rises over the blue glow of Earth's atmosphere.

Earth's atmosphere also protects us from the Sun's heat. It keeps our planet from getting too hot during the day. At night, our atmosphere is like a blanket. It holds in the Sun's heat and keeps the planet from getting too cold.

The Moon does not have this protection. Its daytime temperature is about 253°F (123°C). Its nighttime temperature can get down to −387°F (−233°C). That's much colder than the coldest place on Earth.

Antarctica is the coldest place on Earth. The harsh conditions make it a good place for scientists to test spacecraft. The coldest temperature ever measured there was −129°F (−89°C).

The people of ancient Mexico built the Pyramid of the Moon to honor a moon goddess. They watched the Moon from the pyramid. What are people who study the Moon and space called?

CHAPTER 6
TO THE MOON

Humans have always been curious about the Moon. Long ago, people thought the Moon held special powers. Many cultures prayed to a moon god or goddess.

Astronomers (uh-STRAH-nuh-murz) used telescopes to learn about the Moon. Astronomers are scientists who study outer space. One famous astronomer was Galileo Galilei. He lived about four hundred years ago. Galileo used one of the first telescopes to look at the night sky. He discovered that the Moon has mountains, valleys, and craters.

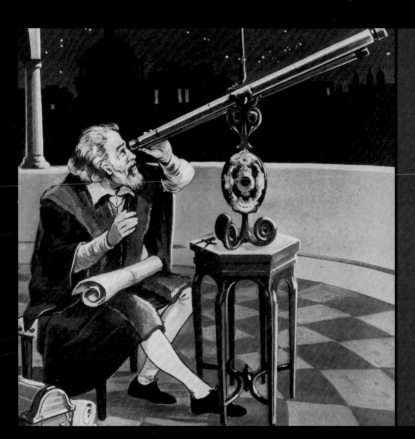

Galileo Galilei was a famous astronomer of the early 1600s. He built his own telescope in 1609.

Other astronomers studied the Moon too.
But they still had many questions. Then people
figured out how to build spacecraft. Spacecraft
are machines that can travel from Earth to
outer space.

Powerful rockets launch
the *Apollo 11* spacecraft
toward the Moon.

Astronauts Neil Armstrong (LEFT), Michael Collins (MIDDLE), and Buzz Aldrin (RIGHT) trained hard for their trip to the Moon.

Some spacecraft carry astronauts (A-struh-nawts). Astronauts are people who travel to outer space. The astronauts Neil Armstrong, Buzz Aldrin, and Michael Collins visited the Moon in 1969. They made history on the Apollo 11 mission.

Neil Armstrong (LEFT) and Buzz Aldrin (RIGHT) plant a U.S. flag on the surface of the Moon during their 1969 visit.

Neil Armstrong and Buzz Aldrin were the first people to walk on the Moon. They had to wear special space suits. The space suits kept the astronauts from getting too hot or too cold.

The astronauts also carried tanks full of oxygen. They needed the oxygen to breathe on the Moon. The astronauts took pictures and collected moon rocks. They helped scientists understand what the Moon is really like.

Buzz Aldrin wears a large oxygen tank on his back while performing research on the surface of the Moon.

Five more Apollo spacecraft landed on the Moon. Each of them carried three more astronauts. The last astronauts visited the Moon in 1972.

Astronaut Harrison Schmitt collects soil samples on the Apollo 17 mission in 1972. He used the lunar roving vehicle at left to travel across the surface of the Moon.

A rocket carrying the *LRO* and *LCROSS* spacecraft awaits launch at the NASA base in Florida.

Other spacecraft have traveled to the Moon since then. But these spacecraft have not carried people. The *LRO* and the *LCROSS* were the latest U.S. spacecraft to go to the Moon. They left Earth in 2009. They are collecting more information about the Moon's surface.

This is an artist's idea of how a future Moon station might look.

The United States hopes to send astronauts
to the Moon in the future. They may try to
build a Moon station. Astronauts could live
in the station for short amounts of time. Then
they could explore more of the Moon.

They might even use the station as a stopping place for bigger journeys. Someday, astronauts might travel from the Moon to other planets. Imagine what they'll discover!

Beyond the Moon, the planet Venus shines like a star.

ON SHARING A BOOK

When you share a book with a child, you show that reading is important. To get the most out of the experience, read in a comfortable, quiet place. Turn off the television and limit other distractions, such as telephone calls. Be prepared to start slowly. Take turns reading parts of this book. Stop occasionally and discuss what you're reading. Talk about the photographs. If the child begins to lose interest, stop reading. When you pick up the book again, revisit the parts you have already read.

BE A VOCABULARY DETECTIVE

The word list on page 5 contains words that are important in understanding the topic of this book. Be word detectives and search for the words as you read the book together. Talk about what the words mean and how they are used in the sentence. Do any of these words have more than one meaning? You will find the words defined in a glossary on page 46.

WHAT ABOUT QUESTIONS?

Use questions to make sure the child understands the information in this book. Here are some suggestions:

What did this paragraph tell us? What does this picture show? What do you think we'll learn about next? What is the Moon's path around Earth called? How long does the Moon take to travel around Earth? Why does Earth's water have tides? What is your favorite part of the book? Why?

If the child has questions, don't hesitate to respond with questions of your own, such as What do *you* think? Why? What is it that you don't know? If the child can't remember certain facts, turn to the index.

INTRODUCING THE INDEX

The index helps readers find information without searching through the whole book. Turn to the index on page 48. Choose an entry such as *solar eclipse,* and ask the child to use the index to find out what causes a solar eclipse. Repeat with as many entries as you like. Ask the child to point out the differences between an index and a glossary. (The index helps readers find information, while the glossary tells readers what words mean.)

THE MOON

BOOKS

Floca, Brian. *Moonshot: The Flight of Apollo 11*. New York: Atheneum Books for Young Readers, 2008. Illustrations help tell the story of the historic mission that put the first men on the Moon.

Jackson, Ellen. *The Worlds around Us*. Minneapolis: Millbrook Press, 2007. This illustrated book is for anyone who wonders what it would be like to visit the Moon and other parts of the solar system.

McNulty, Faith. *If You Decide to Go to the Moon*. New York: Scholastic, 2005. This picture book takes readers on a journey to the Moon with a fictional young boy.

Zemlicka, Shannon. *Neil Armstrong*. Minneapolis: Lerner Publications Company, 2003. The author tells the story of the first human to walk on the Moon.

WEBSITES

Earth's Moon: Kid's Eye View
http://solarsystem.nasa.gov/planets/profilecfm?Object=Moon
&Display=Kids
This website about the Moon is designed just for kids.

NASA Kids' Club
http://www.nasa.gov/audience/forkids/kidsclub/flash/index.html
Learn about space with games, puzzles, and photos from the National Aeronautics and Space Administration.

The Space Place
http://spaceplace.nasa.gov/en/kids/
Go to this Web page of NASA's for more activities, quizzes, and games all about outer space.

GLOSSARY

astronauts (A-struh-nawts): people who explore outer space

astronomers (uh-STRAH-nuh-murz): scientists who study outer space

atmosphere (AT-muhs-feer): the layer of gases that surrounds a planet

axis (AK-sihs): an imaginary line that goes through a planet or moon from top to bottom. A moon spins on its axis.

eclipse (ee-KLIHPS): when a planet or a moon blocks the Sun's light. A lunar eclipse happens when Earth blocks sunlight to the Moon. A solar eclipse happens when the Moon blocks sunlight to Earth.

gravity: a force that pulls one object toward another

orbit: the circular path a planet, moon, or other space object travels in space

phases: shapes of the Moon

rotate (ROH-tayt): to spin around like a top

solar system: the Sun and the group of planets and other objects that travel around it

spacecraft: machines that travel from Earth to outer space

telescope (TEH-luh-skohp): an instrument that makes faraway objects appear bigger and closer

tide: the rise and fall of the world's oceans each day

waning (WAYN-ing) moon: a moon that seems to grow from night to night

waxing moon: a moon that seems to shrink from night to night

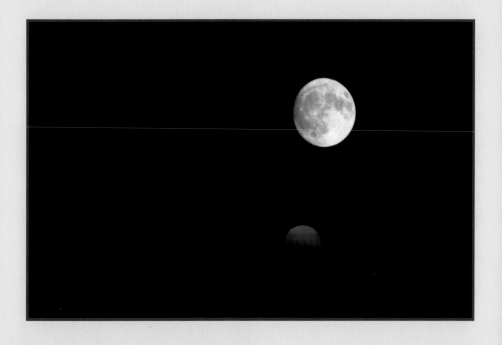

INDEX

Pages listed in **bold** type refer to photographs.